Cultural Traditions in

Germany

Lynn Peppas

Crabtree Publishing Company
www.crabtreebooks.com

Crabtree Publishing Company

www.crabtreebooks.com

Author: Lynn Peppas

Publishing plan research and development:
Reagan Miller

Editor: Rebecca Sjonger, Kelly Spence

Proofreader and indexer: Wendy Scavuzzo

Photo research: Tammy McGarr

Production coordinator and prepress technician:
Tammy McGarr

Print coordinator: Margaret Amy Salter

Cover: Castle Neuschwanstein in the mountains
(background); Traditional Christmas tree (background right);
Boy in lederhosen (right); Young woman in traditional
Bavarian clothes - dirndl or tracht -with a gingerbread
souvenir heart on a festival or Oktoberfest (left); Beer stein
(lower left); Grilled bavarian sausages with sauerkraut
(bottom left); Wiener Schnitzel (bottom); Fresh pretzel
(bottom middle)

Title page: Towers of St. Lorenz Church and central street of
Nuremberg on rainy day in Nuremberg, Bayern Germany

Photographs:

AP Images: Frank Augstein: p10 (bottom)

Getty Images: Ulrich Baumgarten: p29 (bottom right)

Keystone: ©ZUMAPRESS.com/© Frank Rumpenhorst: p6;
©ZUMAPRESS.com/©Matthias Bein: p14;
©ZUMAPRESS.com©Hannibal Hanschke: p29 (top);

Shutterstock: ©Mariia Goloviamko: Title page; ©Pecold: p11;
©Jorg Hackemann: p13 (bottom right); ©ojka: p15; ©abxyz:
p16; ©ETIENjones: p20 (bottom); ©anandoart: p21 (top);
©Bocman1973: p23 (top); Cover (all images), pp 4-5
(background), 7, 8, 9, 10 (inset), 11 (inset), 12, 13 (top left), 15
(bottom right), 17 (bottom), 20 (top), 21 (inset), 22, 23
(bottom), 25 (bottom),
26 (bottom), 27 (bottom right), 30, 31 (background)

Superstock: Römmelt/Mauritius: p17 (top); F1 ONLINE:
p10(top); LOOK-foto: p10 (bottom right)

Thinkstock: Thomas Lohnes/Getty Images: p13; Sean
Gallup/Getty Images): p 24 (middle left); pp 4 (top left);
25 (top), 31 (top right)

Wikimedia Commons: Joseph Karl Stieler: p5 (middle right);
Christl Stef: p18; Praguepower: p24 (bottom); Abmg: p26
(middle right); Immanuel Giel: p27 (top); Bene16: p28

Library and Archives Canada Cataloguing in Publication

Peppas, Lynn, author
    Cultural traditions in Germany / Lynn Peppas.

(Cultural traditions in my world)
Includes index.
Issued in print and electronic formats.
ISBN 978-0-7787-8060-1 (bound).--ISBN 978-0-7787-8065-6 (pbk.).--
ISBN 978-1-4271-9958-4 (pdf).--ISBN 978-1-4271-9953-9 (html)

    1. Holidays--Germany--Juvenile literature. 2. Festivals--Germany--
Juvenile literature. 3. Germany--Social life and customs--Juvenile literature.
I. Title. II. Series: Cultural traditions in my world

GT4850.A2P46 2015   j394.26943   C2014-907785-8
                                      C2014-907786-6

Library of Congress Cataloging-in-Publication Data

Peppas, Lynn.
Cultural traditions in Germany / Lynn Peppas.
    pages cm -- (Cultural traditions in my world)
Includes index.
ISBN 978-0-7787-8060-1 (reinforced library binding) --
ISBN 978-0-7787-8065-6 (pbk.) -- ISBN 978-1-4271-9958-4 (electronic pdf) --
ISBN 978-1-4271-9953-9 (electronic html)
1. Holidays--Germany--Juvenile literature. 2. Germany--Social life and
customs--20th century--Juvenile literature. I. Title.

GT4850.A2P45 2015
394.26094309'04--dc23

                        2014045086

Crabtree Publishing Company

www.crabtreebooks.com   1-800-387-7650

Printed in Canada/042015/EF20150224

Published in Canada
Crabtree Publishing
616 Welland Ave.
St. Catharines, ON
L2M 5V6

Published in the United States
Crabtree Publishing
PMB 59051
350 Fifth Avenue, 59th Floor
New York, New York 10118

Published in the United Kingdom
Crabtree Publishing
Maritime House
Basin Road North, Hove
BN41 1WR

Published in Australia
Crabtree Publishing
3 Charles Street
Coburg North
VIC 3058

Contents

Welcome to Germany

Germany is a large country in central Europe with a **diverse** population of over 80 million people. The country is called *Deutschland* in German, the official language. People speak other languages as well, including Danish, Polish, and Italian. Today, almost one in ten people who live in Germany have moved there from another country.

SCHLESWIG-HOLSTEIN

MECKLENBURG-VORPOMMERN

BREMEN

HAMBURG

BREMEN

NIEDERSACHSEN

BERLIN ■ BERLIN

BRANDENBURG

SACHSEN-ANHALT

NORDRHEIN-WESTFALEN

GERMANY

SACHSEN

THURINGEN

HESSEN

RHEINLAND-PFALZ

SAARLAND

BAYERN

BADEN-WURTTEMBERG

Germany is made up of 16 states and shares its border with nine countries. Berlin is the capital of Germany.

Some customs and traditions in Germany date back thousands of years to ancient Roman times. Others remember important events in Germany's long history. Many celebrations are religious. Most people in Germany are **Christians**. Other Germans follow the **Jewish** or **Muslim** religions.

Did You Know?
Germany is famous for art and science. Classical music composer Ludwig van Beethoven was born in Bonn, Germany, in 1770. Each year in October, Bonn holds a festival in his honor called Beethovenfest.

The Rhine is a large river found in Germany. The river is 865 miles (1,390 kilometers) long and is used for trade and transportation.

Special Days

Germans celebrate family occasions such as birthdays and weddings with family, friends, and big meals. Most of these special days are celebrated the same way as they are in North America. Some of these occasions also include traditions special to Germany. Since the early 1800s, the first day of school has been a special occasion for children. To celebrate this day, parents give their children a decorated paper cone called a *schultüte.* The colorful cone is filled with sweets and new school supplies such as pencils and crayons.

The first day of school is exciting for students in Frankfurt am Main.

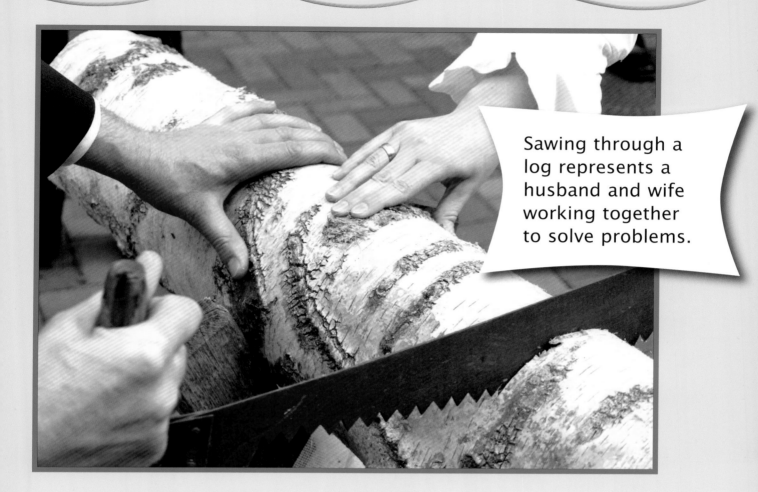

Sawing through a log represents a husband and wife working together to solve problems.

Before a wedding, guests are invited to a party called a *polterabend*. Everyone smashes dishes on the floor. It is believed that the more pieces, the more luck the newlyweds will have. After a wedding, it is also a tradition for a bride and groom to saw through a log together.

Did You Know?
Traditionally, a bride would carry bread and salt on her wedding day to ensure a good **harvest**.

Happy New Year!

In Germany, New Year's Eve is called St. Sylvester's Day, or *Silvester* in German. Lentil soup is a traditional food eaten on this day. Some people believe that each lentil a person eats represents more money in the year to come. It is also believed that eating a marzipan pig will bring a person good luck in the future.

Did You Know?
Sylvester was a Christian **saint** who was buried on December 31 over 1,000 years ago in Rome, Italy.

Bleigiessen is an old New Year's custom in Germany. Melted metal called lead is dropped into a glass of cold water. The shape the metal forms tells a person what the year ahead holds for them.

Brandenburg Gate is a popular place to visit in Berlin. It was built in 1791.

The biggest New Year's celebration takes place in Berlin at Brandenburg Gate. Millions of people join together to celebrate the end of one year and the start of another. Germans enjoy music concerts and fireworks at midnight to welcome the New Year. People wish each other a Happy New Year by saying "*ein gutes neues Jahr!*"

Karneval

Karneval, or Carnival, season kicks off in Germany on November 11 at 11:11 am—two months before most of the celebration's events begin. Karneval began as an ancient festival to keep evil spirits away. Today, it is a time to have fun and eats lots of delicious food before **Lent** begins. In different parts of Germany, Karneval is also known as *Fasching* and *Fastnacht*.

Karneval officially begins on the Thursday before Lent. This day is sometimes called Women's Carnival Day. Women dressed in costumes cut off the bottom of men's ties.

One of the most popular German Karneval celebrations takes place in Cologne. The city has celebrated Karneval since 1823.

Parades, costume balls, and dressing up are all a part of the fun of Karneval in Germany. The festivities end on *Rosenmontag*, or Raging Monday. In Cologne, a parade is held to celebrate the end of the Karneval season.

Did You Know?
Jelly-filled donuts are a popular Karneval treat. Some people play jokes on one another by filling donuts with mustard instead of sweet jelly!

11

Easter

Easter is called *Ostern* in Germany. It is celebrated by some Germans as a Christian holiday. Easter falls on a different day each year between March 21 and April 25.

Did You Know?
Long ago, people believed a German goddess named Eostre brought springtime to Earth. They held festivals to honor the goddess. People believe that the word *Easter* comes from the name *Eostre*.

Painted eggs are a popular Easter tradition that began in Germany hundreds of years ago.

Eostre's favorite animal was a hare or rabbit. The Easter bunny is another tradition that began in Germany, and was brought to North America later.

Frohe Ostern!

Germans decorate eggs and hang them in bushes and trees. Some Germans from the state of Lower Saxony roll or throw painted eggs down hills. The winner is the

egg that gets to the bottom of the hill in one piece! Easter bonfires are also an old tradition that Germans still enjoy today. Long ago, bonfires were believed to scare winter away and welcome spring. Today, they are a good reason to get together and spend time outdoors.

Walpurgis Night and Labor Day

Some Germans celebrate Walpurgis Night on April 30. Hundreds of years ago, some people believed that witches gathered on the Harz Mountains in Germany on this night. People had bonfires to keep the witches away. Today, children sometimes play tricks during Walpurgis Night. They say the witches did it!

Witch dolls are sold as souvenirs at many Walpurgis Night celebrations.

Some Germans show support or protest political issues on Labor Day.

Labor Day or May Day in Germany is celebrated on May 1. Labor Day was first celebrated as a holiday in 1890. Germany joined many other countries in recognizing this day to support people who wanted better working conditions.

Did You Know?
May 1 is also known as Maypole Day in Germany. Long ago, people decorated maypoles on April 30. They stayed up all night to guard it from being stolen by others in nearby towns.

Whit Monday

Whit Monday is a religious holiday that marks the end of Easter. Whit Monday falls 50 days after Easter during Pentecost. Pentecost is a Christian festival that celebrates Jesus' **disciples** and other Christians receiving the Holy Spirit after Jesus died on the cross and rose to Heaven. This holiday is recognized as the time when Jesus' disciples began spreading his holy teachings.

Many German Christians celebrate Whit Monday as the birthday of the Christian church.

The Pentecost ox is an old tradition still celebrated in some areas of Germany. Oxen are dressed with wreaths of flowers to celebrate their first time out to the field after a long winter. In Germany the saying, "primped like a Pentecost ox," means someone is very nicely dressed.

In Germany, a Pentecost tree is usually a birch tree decorated with wreaths and garlands of leaves.

Did You Know?
Long ago, Germans believed that ghosts came out on the night before Whit Monday. Everything was locked up so the ghosts would not steal anything!

Folk and Medieval Festivals

Historical plays and **folk** festivals celebrate German history and culture. The *Drachenstich*, or dragon slaying, festival has been held every August in Furth im Wald for over 400 years. An exciting play **reenacts** the story of a dragon that attacked the town during the Middles Ages.

In 2010, an 11-ton robotic dragon was built for the Drachenstich festival. The dragon is almost 15-feet (4.5 m) tall and walks, roars, spreads its wings, breathes fire, and even bleeds!

A knight dressed in armor on horseback uses a long pole called a lance to knock the other knight off his horse during *Ritterspiele*.

In July, one of the biggest medieval festivals called the *Ritterspiele*, or Knights' Games, is held in Ehrenberg, Germany, in July. Over 10,000 people gather to watch a **tournament** between knights on horseback. The three-day festival includes a parade, music concerts, and fireworks. Actors in costumes also put on a historical reenactment of the Battle of Ehrenberg.

Did You Know?

Germany's *Wurstmarkt* is believed to be the world's oldest folk festival. The 9-day sausage festival held in Bad Dürkheim, Germany, has been held every September for almost 600 years!

DÜRKHEIMER WURSTMARKT

DAS GRÖSSTE WEINFEST DER WELT
2. UND 3. WOCHENENDE IM SEPTEMBER

Oktoberfest

Oktoberfest is a harvest festival. The first Oktoberfest was held in Munich over 200 years ago to celebrate a royal wedding. This 16-day festival begins in September with a parade and ends the first weekend in October. Large tents, rides, and games are set up in a large field called the *Theresienwiese*. Traditional foods such as sauerkraut (pickled cabbage), sausages, pretzels, and strudel are enjoyed at the festival.

Dressing up in traditional clothing is part of the Oktoberfest fun. Men dress in knee-length shorts with suspenders called *lederhosen*. Girls wear colorful dresses called *dirndls*.

Lebkuchenhertz are a popular Oktoberfest tradition. These heart-shaped cookies have different messages written on them and are worn on a ribbon around a person's neck.

Over six million people go to Oktoberfest each year. While the largest celebration takes place in Munich, Oktoberfest is celebrated in cities throughout Germany. The festival is also celebrated in many countries around the world.

Did You Know?
A traditional Oktoberfest drink for adults is beer. Beer is made from a grain called barley. To toast one another, Germans clink their glasses together and say "*Prost!*"

Day of German Unity

After World War Two, Germany was divided in to two separate countries called East Germany and West Germany. On October 3, 1990, they reunited to form one German nation. The Day of German Unity was created as a new national holiday to celebrate the **reunification** of the country.

Did You Know?
For almost 30 years, the Berlin Wall separated East and West Germany. The wall was taken down in 1989. Parts of it still stand today as a memorial.

A Unity Day celebration takes place at Brandenburg Gate in Berlin.

Every year, a national celebration is held in the capital city of a different German state. A *Bürgerfest* is a **citizens'** festival held on this day. In Berlin, Germans celebrate with a four-day festival that includes music, plays, rides, games, and traditional German foods.

German flag colors of gold, red, and black are seen throughout Germany on Unity Day.

23

Thanksgiving and Halloween

Many North American traditions are celebrated in Germany today. Thanksgiving is celebrated as a harvest festival called *Erntedankfest.* This holiday usually falls on the first Sunday in October. Some areas celebrate it on different days in September or October. Some churches hold special thanksgiving services and many towns have celebrations that include music, dancing, and parades.

Germans make harvest crowns and wreaths from stalks of grain. In some towns, a harvest king and queen are crowned.

This tractor is decorated to celebrate a good harvest of crops.

October 31 is also celebrated in Germany as *Reformationstag*, or Reformation Day. It is a day when Martin Luther is remembered for making important changes in the church.

Halloween is a newer holiday celebrated in Germany. Some Germans wear scary costumes and throw Halloween parties on October 31. German children dressed in costumes may go trick-or-treating in large cities, but most save the fun until St. Martin's Day in November.

Did You Know?
Many North Americans traditions are included in German Thanksgiving celebrations. Today, it is common for Germans to enjoy turkey rather than a traditional goose for Thanksgiving dinner.

St. Martin's Day

St. Martin's Day is called *Martinstag* in Germany. It is celebrated on November 11. On this religious day, Germans remember the Christian saint, Martin of Tours.

One famous story about Saint Martin is shown in this painting. Saint Martin is cutting his cloak in half to give to a cold, homeless person.

Did You Know?
Roast goose, red cabbage, and dumplings is a traditional meal on St. Martin's Day. The goose is a popular symbol of St. Martin because he once hid in a barn full of geese!

A lantern is a small light with a paper case or covering. It has a handle and can be carried by hand.

Often, German children buy or make a lantern for St. Martin's Day. Children parade through the streets carrying lanterns at night on November 11. Sometimes they are led by a person dressed as St. Martin in a red cape. In some areas, children go door-to-door singing Martinstag songs in return for sweets.

Bonfires are also a popular activity on St. Martin's Day.

National Day of Mourning

The National Day of **Mourning** in Germany is held on the Sunday closest to November 16. It is a silent holiday in Germany. This means that on this day, music and dancing are not allowed by law in some German states. It is sometimes also called German Remembrance Sunday. It was first held in 1922 to remember German soldiers who died during World War One. Today Germans remember and honor people who died in all wars.

Wreaths are placed at a memorial for German soldiers who died in World War One and World War Two.

On the National Day of Mourning, the German president gives a speech to honor all people who were unfairly treated by their government or who died in war.

Deutscher Bundestag

Special remembrance ceremonies take place across Germany. The country's national anthem and a **patriotic** song called "The Good Comrade" are often played. *Comrade* means "close friend." This song is also traditionally played at military funerals. Many people also visit cemeteries to remember loved ones on this day.

Did You Know?

Germany's National Day of Mourning was held in February until 1945. It was then moved to November. November is a common month around the world to remember those who died in times of war.

St. Nikolaus Day and Christmas

Each year, Germans celebrate the joyful Christmas season all through December. On December 5 and 6, people celebrate St. Nikolaus Day. During the night, boys and girls leave empty boots and shoes by the front door. A visit from St. Nikolaus will fill the shoes of well-behaved children with sweets and presents. If a child has not behaved well, they might find a tree branch or lump of coal in their shoe instead!

Did You Know?
In Germany, St. Nikolaus has a helper named *Knecht Ruprecht*, or Servant Rupert.

Christmas markets, or *Christkindlmarkts*, have been a German holiday tradition for over 700 years. People visit the markets to buy handmade crafts, listen to music, and eat traditional holiday treats such as gingerbread and sausages. Most Christmas markets in Germany open during the **Advent** season. On December 25, Christmas Day is celebrated with family and friends. A traditional meal of goose or carp, a fresh water fish, is eaten.

Advent calendars are a German tradition. Each one has 25 windows to be opened, one for each day in December until Christmas. Behind every window is a Christmas picture or treat.

This brightly lit Christmas market is in Frankfurt am Main.

Glossary

Advent The season beginning four Sundays before Christmas

Christian Someone who follows the teachings of Jesus Christ, whom they believe to be the Son of God

citizen A person who lives in a town or city

disciple A follower of Jesus Christ

diverse Different from one another

folk Relating or originating from a certain group of people or region

harvest The season when crops are gathered

Jewish People who follow the teachings of God and the Old Testament in the Bible

Lent A period of fasting and regret for one's sins during the 40 days from Ash Wednesday to Easter

mourning Feeling or showing grief after someone's death or another loss

Muslim People who follow Islam and the teachings of the prophet Muhammad

patriotic Showing love for one's country

reenact To perform again

reunification The process during which East and West Germany became one country

saint A holy person

tournament A contest of skill and courage between knights wearing armor and fighting with lances or swords

Index